Betty Bonnet's Camp-Fire

February 1917

Plate 1

NOTE—If the whole page is mounted on muslin or linen before the figures are cut out the different parts will last longer and the tabs will not tear so easily. Cut along the dotted lines, and slip the doll's head into the slits thus made. By pasting an inch-wide strip of cardboard at the waistline, slightly bent to form an easel, the doll can be made to stand.

Betty Bonnet's Country Cousins

March 1917

Plate 2

NOTE — If the whole page is mounted on muslin or linen before the figures are cut out the different parts will last longer and the tabs will not tear so easily. Cut along the dotted lines, and slip the doll's head
into the slits thus made. By pasting an inch-wide strip of cardboard at the waistline, slightly bent to form an easel, the doll can be made to stand.

Betty Bonnet's Big Brother

May 1917

Plate 3

Betty Bonnet's College Cousins

June 1917

Plate 4

NOTE—If the whole page is mounted on muslin or linen before the figures are cut out the different parts will last longer and the tabs will not tear so easily. Cut along the dotted lines in hats, and slip the doll's head into the slits thus made. By pasting an inch-wide strip of cardboard at the waistline, slightly bent to form an easel, the doll can be made to stand.

Betty Bonnet's Patriotic Party

July 1917

Plate 5

NOTE — If the whole page is mounted on muslin or linen before the figures are cut out the different parts will last longer and the tabs will not tear so easily. Cut along the dotted lines, and slip the doll's head into the slits thus made. By pasting an inch-wide strip of cardboard at the waistline, slightly bent to form an easel, the doll can be made to stand.

Betty Bonnet's Grandparents
Now and Long Ago

September 1917

Plate 6

NOTE—If the whole page is mounted on muslin or linen before the figures are cut out the different parts will last longer and the tabs will not tear so easily. Cut along the dotted lines, and slip the doll's head into the slits thus made. By pasting an inch-wide strip of cardboard at the waistline, slightly bent to form an easel, the doll can be made to stand.

Betty Bonnet's Army and Navy Cousins

November 1917

Plate 7

NOTE — If the whole page is mounted on muslin or linen before the figures are cut out the different parts will last longer and the tabs will not tear so easily. Cut along the dotted lines, and slip the doll's head into the slits thus made. By pasting an inch-wide strip of cardboard at the waistline, slightly bent to form an easel, the doll can be made to stand.

Betty Bonnet Shops Early

December 1917

Plate 8

NOTE — If the whole page is mounted on muslin or linen before the figures are cut out the different parts will last longer and the tabs will not tear so easily. Cut along the dotted lines in hats, and slip the doll's head into the slits thus made. By pasting an inch-wide strip of cardboard at the waistline, slightly bent to form an easel, the doll can be made to stand.

Betty Bonnet's New Year's Callers

January 1918

Plate 9

NOTE — If the whole page is mounted on muslin or linen before the figures are cut out the different parts will last longer and the tabs will not tear so easily. Cut along the dotted lines in hats, and slip the doll's head into the slits thus made. By pasting an inch-wide strip of cardboard at the waistline, slightly bent to form an easel, the doll can be made to stand.

Betty Bonnet's Valentine

Plate 10

NOTE — If the whole page is mounted on muslin or linen before the figures are cut out the different parts will last longer and the tabs will not tear so easily. Cut along the dotted lines in hats, and slip the doll's head into the slits thus made. By pasting an inch-wide strip of cardboard at the waistline, slightly bent to form an easel, the doll can be made to stand.

Betty Bonnet's Household Servants

March 1918

Plate 11

NOTE—If the whole page is mounted on muslin or linen before the figures are cut out the different parts wil! last longer and the tabs will not tear so easily. By pasting an inch-wide strip of cardboard at the waistline, slightly bent to form an easel, the doll can be made to stand.

Betty Bonnet's Rainy Day Party

April 1918

Plate 12

NOTE — If the whole page is mounted on muslin or linen before the figures are cut out the different parts will last longer and the tabs will not tear so easily. Cut along the dotted lines in hats, and slip the doll's head into the slits thus made. By pasting an inch-wide strip of cardboard at the waistline, slightly bent to form an easel, the doll can be made to stand.

Betty Bonnet's May Basket

May 1918

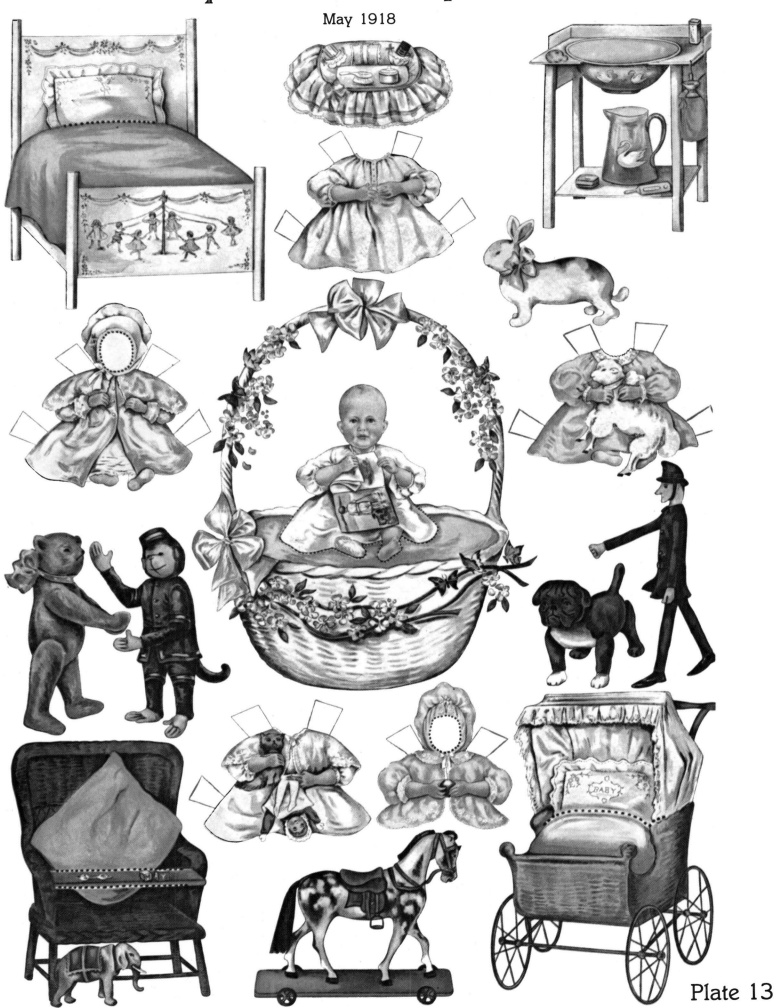

Plate 13

NOTE—If the whole page is mounted on muslin or linen before the figures are cut out the different parts will last longer and the tabs will not tear so easily. Cut along the dotted lines, and slip the doll's head into the slits thus made. By pasting an inch-wide strip of cardboard at the waistline, slightly bent to form an easel, the doll can be made to stand.

Betty Bonnet Goes to a Wedding

The Bride   June 1918

Plate 14

Betty Bonnet Goes to a Wedding

The Bridegroom   July 1918

Plate 15

NOTE — If the whole page is mounted on muslin or linen before the figures are cut out the different parts will last longer and the tabs will not tear so easily. Cut along the dotted lines in hats, and slip the doll's head into the slits thus made. By pasting an inch-wide strip of cardboard at the waistline, slightly bent to form an easel, the doll can be made to stand.

Betty Bonnet Goes to a Wedding

The Page and the Flower Girl   September 1918

Plate 16

NOTE—If the whole page is mounted on muslin or linen before the figures are cut out the different parts will last longer and the tabs will not tear so easily. Cut along the dotted lines in hats, and slip the doll's head into the slits thus made. By pasting an inch-wide strip of cardboard at the waistline, slightly bent to form an easel, the doll can be made to stand.